Sept '95   PADSTOW

CW00376420

NORTH CORNWALL RE

Hilda Hambly

BOSSINEY BOOKS

First published in 1992 by Bossiney Books,
St Teath, Bodmin, Cornwall.

Typeset and printed by
Penwell Print Ltd, Callington, Cornwall.

© HILDA HAMBLY

ISBN 0 948158 79 4

ACKNOWLEDGEMENTS

Front cover design: MAGGIE GINGER

Modern photographs: RAY BISHOP

*The author thanks everyone who has helped
and especially her daughter Margaret and Ray Bishop
for their particular support.*

NORTH CORNWALL REFLECTIONS

FLANKED BY the sea on the north and south and almost completely cut off from England by the River Tamar, Cornwall is very nearly an island. Cornwall is different – a land apart – and North Cornwall, rich in his history and soaked in legend, underlines that very quality.

There is a wonderful diversity here in North Cornwall: hamlets and towns, almost forgotten railway lines and an airfield on Bodmin Moor, small fishing villages on the coast and a major British holiday resort in Newquay, narrow twisting country lanes and fast modern roads. It is difficult to say North Cornwall is this or that, and the pictures and words inside these pages confirm that diversity.

The camera – or more accurately the woman or the man holding it – can do a whole range of things: record or probe, identify or analyse. Above all, the camera is the *reliable* witness.

Memory and the camera are quite different. Our memory is highly selective; we *think* we recall the essentials but often our memory magnifies or even distorts. But the camera, in the right hands, records *all*. The photograph may be simply a vase of flowers or a wide stretch of landscape across Bodmin Moor. In both pictures we get the whole scene: the small and the broad.

Looking at some of these old photographs, we are reminded of that basic truth. Furthermore we understand now that many of those early photographers were truly camera artists.

Here is a rich harvest of photographs, nearly all old and many appearing in book form for the first time. They *reflect* North Cornwall, showing the region at work and in recreation.

They not only turn the calendars back, they remind us of the challenge ahead: the need to preserve. Travelling from page to page on this North Cornwall journey is an experience in nostalgia, but worrying too in that we clearly see how much of North Cornwall has been changed – and gone for ever.

But in Hilda Hambly we have a guide in words and pictures

THE AUTHOR inside her cottage in Eddystone Terrace, Wadebridge. Alongside her is a fine display of royal plates and mugs. 'I left home to live and work in Wadebridge when I was fourteen years old.'

MR COCK with his delivery vans and horses outside his bakery and restaurant in Egloshayle Road, Wadebridge around 1920. Even today this spot is known locally as Cock's Corner.

who cares about North Cornwall – cares about the people and the place. A member of the Old Cornwall Society and a honorary member of the Wadebridge Camera Club, she feels strongly about Cornwall and she thinks Cornish. Anyone who heard her being interviewed by Daphne Skinnard on BBC Radio Cornwall in November 1991 will know that.

Admittedly Daphne Skinnard is an intelligent skilful interviewer, but it was a remarkable radio debut for a lady who was born as long ago as 1910.

Hilda gathers her knowledge in various ways. She has a natural thirst for the past. She enjoys reading Cornish history, visiting places and listening to talks, but she loves talking about the old days to local people best of all, and, not least, she uses old pictures as a means of exploring earlier times. Her native curiosity enables her to understand the full picture.

Hilda has had a lifelong passion for photographs.

Our Victorian and Edwardian forebears were keen collectors too, and not just of the saucy seaside postcards. In the main they went for topographical views – and it is the same today. You go to an auction room and an album of old photographs or picture postcards will often fetch a good price – many times their original value.

Hilda's slide shows have become part of the North Cornwall scene. She is quite simply a natural communicator, rattling off facts and figures without a note. She has a fund of stories.

'There was the Wadebridge man who walked to St Breward to work on a farm when the threshing machine was harvesting. however the weather became wet and windy: so the farmer said "You can stay the night." The man said "Thank you very much" but later was seen putting on his coat. "What are you doing?" asked the farmer. "I must pop home to tell the Missus," said the Wadebridge man.

'One day the same Wadebridge character was walking home, when he got to Egloshayle Church he decided to light his pipe. There was a strong wind blowing into his face; so he turned round to light his pipe, but forgot to turn back until he got to the town of Bodmin!"

Such is the skill of Hilda's commentary on these occasions, you begin to wonder about that old saying 'Every picture tells a story'. The truth is Hilda often has a story behind the picture – and usually a very good story. I have attended one of her slide shows and there were times that evening when you could have heard the proverbial pin drop. But she is a two-way communicator and positively encourages comments from the gathering.

Hilda is quite an all-rounder: more than just a collector of old

A SMALL boy enjoys the view. Pawton Quoit is the name on many maps, but many of us Cornish folk prefer its other name, the Giant's Quoit. A burial chamber, it lies two miles south-west of Wadebridge on St Breock's Downs. Less known than Trevethy on Bodmin Moor or Lanyon Down in Penwith, it is nevertheless a remarkable feature in the landscape.

photographs, she is an accomplished photographer, the winner of a number of awards, an excellent cook, a loyal supporter of the Royal family – there's no doubt which side she would have taken in the Civil War. She is also a generous character; learning that I am a collector of autographs, she presented me with some music autographed by Sir Arthur Sullivan.

It was in November 1991 that Hilda Hambly made her debut for Bossiney with *Old North Cornwall*: a book which immediately won high praise and broke all book sale records in her home town of Wadebridge. Nancy Hammonds, reviewing it in the *Evening Herald*, said: *'Hilda Hambly proves it's never too late to write that book . . . Born in Trevia near Camelford, Mrs Hambly, at 81, has her first book* Old North Cornwall *just published by Bossiney . . . She will turn back the clock for any reader as she reflects on a way of life forever gone. It is a treasure chest of nostalgia, just in time for Christmas.'*

Ronnie Hoyle, writing on the Books Page of *The Western Morning News*, evoked the spirit of that first book: *'Now she has put her collection together to produce her first book . . . to turn the clock back half a century or more, to the days before the mass intrusion of cars, when the fastest thing was a horse, a train or maybe the old charabanc.*

'An array of pictures and people, places and events pepper the pages of this nostalgic memoir as she shares her collection for the first time – but don't worry, Hilda still has many more photographs in her collection which have not seen the light of day yet, so a second book could quite easily come our way.'

This book then is the fulfilment of that forecast.

THE DUKE of Windsor being driven through Wadebridge in the 1930s, before the controversy of his abdication. The Duke made a number of visits to North Cornwall over the years, including a holiday at the Headland Hotel, Newquay, when he was convalescing from measles caught at the Royal Naval College, Dartmouth. He also visited the Tangye family home at Glendorgal.

THE OLD Cornwall Society annual bonfire on St Breock Downs 1981, when, as the Lady of Flowers, I threw the bunch of good and bad flowers and herbs on the fire at the appropriate moment in the service. The tradition of Midsummer bonfires has in recent years, been re-introduced, especially here in Cornwall where, on the 23rd night of June hill-top fires can be seen blazing across the countryside. The holder of the symbolic bunch of flowers and bad herbs wishes that every good one shall spring a thousandfold, and every bad one be destroyed, by virtue of the fire.

In June 1992 Bossiney celebrated 17 years of full time publishing, and Tom Salmon, former head of BBC radio and television at Plymouth kindly sent me a note: 'Congratulations on your 17th. Cornwall owes you much for encompassing things which but for you would have been lost.' Sonia and I appreciated those warm words, and nothing personifies that philosophy better than Hilda Hambly's books.

Sprightly and still going strong at 82, she is a mine of information on North Cornwall and Wadebridge in particular. As St Ives is the window of his world for the Cornish painter Bryan Pearce, so Wadebridge is for Hilda. But on this trip down memory lane, she takes us to a wide range of locations in her beloved North Cornwall: from St Columb to beyond Bude, from Tintagel across to the moor to the old county town of Bodmin – and elsewhere.

I am at my desk just outside St Teath early on a summer morning, and scattered over this desk are Hilda's words and photographs. They are a joy and in spirit they take me to other places – and other times.

Michael Williams
June 1992

A SIGNING session at the Wadebridge Bookshop in November 1991 when the author presented a copy of her book Old North Cornwall *to the Mayor of Wadebridge. Left to right: publisher Michael Williams, Hilda Hambly, Ivan Fisher, the Mayor of Wadebridge, and Betty Rickard of the Wadebridge Bookshop.*

THIS OLD photograph shows how parts of Wadebridge have been transformed. Here we see advertisements for Woolcock, agent to the Great Western Railway – and furniture remover. The same firm also provided greys for weddings and a modern glass hearse for funerals. The transformation is that Woolcock's establishment is no longer here – instead on the very same spot we have Wadebridge post office.

CHIEF INSPECTOR Daniel Adolphus Miller flanked by two constables – I guess this was then the entire police force for Wadebridge. Chief Inspector Miller, who was born in 1859 and died in 1947, came to the town from St Columb: the very first inspector. He arrested a man for poaching rabbits and said to him 'Do you want my punishment, or do you want to go to court?' The man replied 'I will take your punishment, please, sir.' Later he was told to go home and 'take the rabbits because your family must be starving.'

THIS PHOTOGRAPH of the Allen family of Wadebridge is typical of many taken at the beginning of the first World War when the eldest sons were going to serve their country. Sadly, the second son in this family never returned. There was also another son, Frankie, who died aged three. This was therefore the complete family: 11 children in all. Twenty-two years of having children – and when these were older three more were fostered and reared within the family circle: Joan, now Mrs Goudge of St Stephens, the Lyford twins, Peter now deceased and John of Bodmin, will always remain members of the Allen family, not in name but by the love and affection that tie people together for ever.

Here is the family portrait which now hangs in my Wadebridge home – the parents were Annie – nee May formerly of St Columb – and James Allen. In this picture the individuals are as follows: Back row left to right: May, who married Charles Brenton (two daughters), Stanley, who was killed in the war, Bill, who married Annie Brenton, sister of Charlie, Violet, who married Charlie Hurrell (one son).

Front row: Bert, my first husband (one son and one daughter), Annie Allen, Fred, who married Violet Irons, (two sons and two daughters), Jimmy Allen, Percy, died aged 21, Emmie, sat on her mother's knee – her first husband was Sidney Margerrison by whom she had three daughters, and her second husband was Ken Thomas, (one son), and alongside, Eddie, who married Joyce Brenton (one daughter and one son), and Hilda, who married Dennis Latcham (two sons), who is the only survivor of the Allen family – Eddie and Emmie having died in 1990, within two weeks of each other. The sadness of the loss can never take away the happiness of the memories of the wonderful times we shared and the joy of the 17 grandchildren who followed.

St. Breock Village.

▲ *ST BREOCK Village. This is one of my favourite villages in North Cornwall and I am glad to see it is relatively unchanged. It is roughly one mile west of Wadebridge, and has a beautiful church and churchyard. There is an interesting tombstone at St Breock which reads: 'Here lyeth buried John Tregeagle of Trevorder, Esq.' the year being 1679. This commemorates the son of Jan Tregeagle whose endless task was to empty Dozmary Pool, out on Bodmin Moor, with a leaky limpet shell. The tombstone is among others at the east end of the south aisle. Jan's own tombstone has never been found although his burial in 1655 is recorded in the church register.*

COTTAGES AT Polmorla village on the outskirts of Wadebridge on the road to St Breock. This old photograph stirs our curiosity. The white look of the road suggests a light fall of snow, but there is no hint of snow in the countryside behind the cottages. It's certainly winter – with smoke coming from the chimneys. Were the three figures in the picture posing for the photographer? Or did he just happen along and use them? ▼

ME AT THE age of 17 photographed by Mr J.B. Wills of Wadebridge who owned the Cosy Cafe, and was well known for his photography. He was known locally as Mr Cosy, and staged silent films in Wadebridge Town Hall on Friday and Saturday evenings. This shot of me was taken in his studio above the Cosy Cafe.

WADEBRIDGE MALE Voice Choir about to set off for their annual outing. The gentleman in the foreground is Dr Wilson Gunn, their conductor. He was the local doctor and his wife Daisy composed music. They lived at Riverside House, by the bridge; the front of their house faced the river. But it's since been completely demolished.

SONG

WELCOME TO SPRING

Words & Music by
DAISY WILSON GUNN

COPYRIGHT

PRICE 2/- NETT.

GLASGOW,
J. B. GALBRAITH & SON,
10 RENFIELD STREET.

LONDON : WEEKES & Cº.
14 Hanover Street, Regent St., W

WELCOME TO SPRING.

DAISY WILSON GUNN.

Daff-o-dils are dancing in the breeze, Blossoms pink and white are on the trees,

Lit-tle lambs are play-ing, Lovers are a - may ing, To each o-ther telling. "Spring has come;"

CONCERT

BY

The Wadebridge Male Voice Choir,

ASSISTED BY

Wadebridge Amateur Orchestra,

IN THE

Town Hall, Wadebridge, January 3rd, 1923,

At 7.30 p.m.   Doors open at 7 p.m.

SOLOISTS:

Soprano—Mrs. RONALD RAY (Miss V. EUSTACE),

Violin—Miss PEDLAR,

Tenor—Mr. STUART LOCKETT,

Bass — Mr. A. B. HAWKE.

Accompanists—Miss HILDA HOSKIN and Mr. A. ROBERTS.

Hon. Conductor—Dr. WILSON-GUNN.

R. E. DUNN, Hon. Treasurer.
A. ROBERTS, Hon. Secretary.

Quintrell & Co., Wadebridge.

MR FRANK MALLETT, owner of the ironmonger's shop in Molesworth Street. He was very musical and took the female lead in the plays he produced at the Wadebridge Town Hall. His enthusiasm for the theatre was such that he went up to London to see the Gilbert and Sullivan shows. Those, of course, were the days when people had to make their own entertainment, and, looking back, it's incredible how much the villages and the towns of North Cornwall did in the way of plays and musical concerts. ▼

▲

THE WADEBRIDGE Male Voice Choir had a wide repertoire - not only did they sing the compositions of their conductor's wife Daisy Wilson Gunn as depicted on the preceding pages – but, backed by the town's orchestra, they entertained with Victorian ballads, traditional songs and Gilbert and Sullivan. At this town hall concert in 1923 there were 19 items, including extracts from HMS Pinafore, Blue Butterflies sung by Mrs Ronald Ray, several part songs, two violin solos and a rousing grand march from the orchestra to round off the evening.

NANNY MOORE'S Bridge, a well-known Bude landmark. One travel writer referred to '. . . an ancient device of stone and wood, known as Nanny Moore's Bridge.' This good lady lived in a nearby cottage, and the river which flows into the sea at Bude is the Neet.

A DELIGHTFUL card: the coach and horses stopping at Kilkhampton, outside the London Inn, watched by the local policeman. Today this fast road linking North Cornwall to North Devon takes thousands and thousands of cars. In the background is Kilkhampton Church; the great Purcell played the organ here. That church tower is a landmark for many miles; it stands some 400 feet above sea level.

THE FALCON HOTEL, on the southern side of the Bude Canal, is a splendid example of an old stage coach inn. Built by the Acland family, it's reputed to be the oldest coaching house in all North Cornwall. Its name – The Falcon – comes from the falcon which tops the family crest of the Aclands.

COOMBE VALLEY Mill near Bude. The original of the postcard was in sepia – once a very fashionable colour for cards. This is the heart of Hawker Country. Robert Stephen Hawker was squire and parson hereabouts for 41 years. He was an author and poet, a man of many roles, and gained immortality in Cornwall with the lines depicted, in his own handwriting, below and opposite.

HERE IS some historic Cornish handwriting made available to Bossiney by the Cornish Studies Library at Redruth. These pages concern Robert Stephen Hawker's famous ballad The Song of the Western Men. *The strength and willpower of Parson Hawker shine from these lines. For many of us Cornish people this is the Cornish national anthem. The singing of these words at a Cornwall Rugby match is a big part of the occasion.*

The Song
of the Western Men.

I

A good Sword and a trusty Hand!
A merry Heart and true!—
King James his men shall understand
What Cornish Lads can do!

II

And have they fix'd the where and when?
And shall Trelawny die?
Here's Twenty Thous-and Cornish men
Will know the reason why!

III

Out spake their Captain brave and bold,—
A merry Wight was he,—
If London Tower were Michael's Hold
We'll set Trelawny free!
And have &c

ROUGH SEAS at Bude. This dramatic seascape was used to promote The Western Daily Mercury *as the 'best morning paper in the district.'*

Photo by   SEA AT BUDE, NORTH CORNWALL.   Thorn, Bude.
The "Western Daily Mercury" is the Best Morning Paper in this district.

IV

We'll cross the Tamar, Land to Land!
    The Severn is no stay:
All side by side, and hand to hand,
    And who shall bid us Nay?
                  And have &c

V

And when we come to London Wall,
    A pleasant Sight to view, —
Come forth! Come forth! ye Cowards all!
    Here's men as good as you!
                  And have &c

VI

Trelawny He's in Keep and Hold,
    Trelawny He may die:
But here's Twenty Thousand Bold
    Will know the reason why!
              R.S.H.

21

Medrose, Delabole, R. S. O. Cornwall.
T. Harris's Series, Quethiock, Liskeard.

ARTHUR MEE once said: 'There is nothing else in Cornwall like Old Delabole . . . They were taking slates from here when Shakespeare was writing Hamlet, when Drake was driving the Armada off the seas.' Here is one of the most remarkable basins in all Britain, from which millions of slates have been brought up – going on the roofs of houses, into walls of buildings and in churchyards as tombstones. One sad local story concerns a girl who took her father's dinner to the quarry long ago. The girl was at the top of the quarry when a sudden landslide came – and she had no father. He was buried in the landslide.

These two cards portray different faces of the old quarrying village. The top card is of the Medrose area of Delabole – it is just possible that some of these young children are now elderly residents. They are all concentrating on the photographer and his camera. The lower card is of the Delabole Slate Quarries. In the heyday of quarrying many visitors were surprised to see the astonishing heap of slate thrown away – for every decent piece of slate there were many bad ones. Over the years hundreds of thousands of tons of slate must have been brought up. Both these postcards were published by T. Harris of Quethiock, Liskeard.

The Grove & Pappet Heads, Old Delabole Slate Quarries, R. S. O. Cornwall.
T. Harris's Series, Quethiock, Liskeard.

MAYPOLE IN 1922, when Enfield Park was opened in the town of Camelford. It would have been a memorable day for these young girls, all of whom would now be senior citizens.

CAMELFORD IN more leisurely days. This card was despatched from the White Hart, Launceston, on March 7 1921. Cecil, writing to Mrs Pascoe of Gerrards Cross, Bucks, says 'Got here (Launceston) at 6-30 this evening. From Camelford we made a detour round by Tintagel for tea. Sunny all day long. Left PZ at 11-15.' I would have been eleven years old and attending the school at Camelford.

MY YOUNGEST brother Derek, aged probably four or five, by the village pump in the days when we lived at Trevia, near Camelford. We all fetched our water from this pump and, as a family, lived for some years in the house in the background.

From the Western Morning News, Dec 22, 1932:

A FIRE which totally destroyed a Post Office, telephone exchange, and large general store occurred in the main street of Camelford in the early hour s of December 22 1932.

There was no loss of life, but injuries were sustained by one man, on whom a part of the front of the building fell as he was trying to save some of the furniture.

As a result of the telephonic facilities being disturbed, Camelford was cut off from communications.

The fire obtained a firm hold on the premises before the arrival of Bodmin Fire Brigade. Indeed, when the brigade reached the scene they found the property almost burnt to the ground and concentrated their efforts to confining the blaze to the building and preventing it spreading to the Methodist Chapel on one side and the Inn on the other. Vans containing mailbags were speedily removed from a garage at the rear of the burning buildings but some Christmas post was destroyed.

An occupant of the living rooms over the post office and stores was rescued by a youth after climbing out of a window on to the roof of the Inn. She was the daughter of the postmaster, Miss Hilda Haddy. Other occupants of the house were Mr & Mrs William Haddy the proprietor of the stores, his wife and a Miss Long, they escaped by the rear of the premises.

◀ *WEDDING PHOTOGRAPHS have long been important features of family albums. This wedding photograph taken in 1904 is of Mr & Mrs Saltern, at the Methodist Chapel, Camelford. Mr Saltern ran a taxi service from his home in Chapel Street; his mother, standing on the left, was Nurse Saltern who worked in the Camelford Workhouse, the building now made into flats.*

MINSTER CHURCH near Boscastle. The mother church of Boscastle, whether you approach on foot through Minster Woods or from the lane linking Boscastle and Lesnewth, it comes as a delightful surprise. Here you will find an unsolved North Cornish mystery: the pair of scissors carved halfway up the western face of the church tower. Nobody knows their origin or purpose.

Boscastle. Minster Church.

THERE IS in Boscastle just a hint of Clovelly in North Devon – as these white-faced cottages confirm. You'll find some really beautiful cottages in the village: Cornish homes, planned by necessity and built by local skill and craft. Of course, over the years, more and more buildings have been constructed, but there remain corners of Boscastle which have hardly changed.

ANOTHER DELIGHTFUL card from Boscastle, and posted from there to St Endellion in the year 1904. The brief message on the back reads: 'Hope you will like this card. Have you had any like it before? With love U.W.T.' Doubtless one card collector writing to another.

27

BOSCASTLE
FLORAL DANCE

4/113

HELSTON MAY be the most famous Floral Dance. But here are two pictures proving that Boscastle is proud of its own traditional Dance. Here the photographer has caught the procession as it comes down the hill and passes the Wellington Hotel. This is the foot of the Old Road, and the hotel was originally known as the Bos Castle. Boscastle was an early destination on the tourist route of North Cornwall. A guide, published in 1908, described The Wellington as 'High-class' family and tourist hotel and coaching house – romantic scenery, bracing air, magnificent cliffs and lovely valleys.'

The photograph opposite, top, is a more general shot of the lower part of the village with The Wellington on the left of the Old Road. 'Boscastle is the warmest, most sheltered, most verdant place along the north coast,' wrote the editor in that same 1908 guide.

Boscastle

CRACKINGTON HAVEN, probably an early picture postcard photographed from the air. 'A romantic spot, with cliffs towering on either side' said an old guide book to North Cornwall. The early motorists, visitors especially, must have driven down into the Haven with care, it being 1 in 6 steep, and winding.

▼

CRACKINGTON HAVEN.

COTTAGES MUST be among the most photographed and painted subjects in our Cornish villages. Here is a fourteenth century cottage at Tintagel. This postcard was posted at Tintagel and sent to a Miss M. Richards in Sidcup, Kent. It reads: 'Just a card to let you know we are having a nice time but so far the weather is somewhat rough – we are hoping for the wind to drop.' These holiday sentiments must have been expressed in many postcards despatched from Tintagel which faces the Atlantic.

KING ARTHUR's Castle Hotel on the cliffs at Tintagel. Standing on land once known as Fire Beacon and constructed in castellated style, it was opened in 1899, the year the South African war began. Sir Noel Coward stayed here. From the hotel you have magnificent views of the ruins of Tintagel Castle. There can be few finer views from any hotel in the whole of the West Country. Nearby is Barras Head, still known as Barras Nose on some maps. The National Trust acquired Barras as long ago as 1897 – only their second capture.

AN INSIDE shot of King Arthur's Hotel: the dining room. It looks attractive, but Maud, the sender of this card in August 1905, probably never came back to Cornwall. '… weather atrocious … G is not favourably impressed with Cornwall … too cold and wet all the time.' That, of course, is an unfair generalization. Maud seemed unhappy about life in general. 'Excuse this card … can't see another one.' Today we, who collect old cards and photographs, would rate it a real collector's item. In fact Maud would be astonished to discover the value of this card has probably increased 200% since that August day in Tintagel.

KING ARTHUR'S
CASTLE HOTEL,
TINTAGEL,
CORNWALL.
(Dining Room.)

HERE IS a delightful picnic party on a North Cornish beach: all six characters posing quite deliberately for the photographer. The ladies had brought their hats – and the teapot! The two boys proudly display their fishing nets, their short trousers have been rolled up enabling them to go into the deepest of pools or maybe even venture into the sea itself. The little girl, wearing her shoes, presumably was not allowed into the water.

FISHING HAS long been one of Cornwall's major industries, and this card of Cornish fishermen mending their nets could have been a scene at Padstow or Port Isaac – or a whole range of places along our North Cornish coast. This card, despatched from Cornwall in October 1909, complains about the weather – and Grandma has had a bad cold!

THE CUTTING of the last few handfuls of the standing corn in the harvest field was marked by a pagan ceremony known as 'Crying the neck', as the reaper severed the last swath and raised it high above his head, people would shout. 'We 'av 'n! We 'av 'n! We 'av 'n!' The reply would be ' A neck! A neck! A neck!' Everyone would cheer. The Old Cornwall Society has revived this custom and a service, in the Cornish language, is held in the nearest church to give thanks for the harvest. Our picture shows Mr Morton-Nance of Padstow at St Endellion.

Launching the Lifeboat   Padstow

TWO DIFFERENT pictures of lifeboat service in North Cornwall. The top photograph, taken on the Rock side of the estuary, is of horses drawing the lifeboat out into the sea – note the lady spectators in their smart Edwardian hats. The lower picture is one of equality: men and women launching the Padstow lifeboat. Great deeds of heroism have been performed along this treacherous coat of North Cornwall.

AN EXCELLENT example of the camera craft of Herbert Hughes – this time at Marsland Mouth, taken in July 1913. This is an unusual photograph in that the two gentlemen are shaking hands across the Cornwall-Devon border. It also portrays the beautiful but wicked qualities of this northern coastline. Little wonder that such a stretch of coast has been the graveyard of so many ships.

Cornish Fisherwomen

I DO NOT know from which port these Cornish fisherwomen came, but I do know they had a very tough life. They were marvellous models for the photographers and the painters – and they would have had some grand tales to tell.

Dolphin Street, Port Isaac

PORT ISAAC is another of my favourite North Cornwall villages. This card, dating from the reign of King Edward, is of Dolphin Street with the Dolphin Inn in the background. Today Port Isaac attracts thousands of visitors, but when this photograph was taken tourism was only beginning. This card, despatched from Port Isaac, is addressed to a Miss Hawken in Plymouth, and simply says 'Coming tomorrow night.' This says a great deal about the speed and the reliability of the Post Office in those days – moreover the postage stamp cost just half a penny!

St. Michael's Church, Rock.

FRITH.
RK.14.

◀

HERE IS a picture postcard publisher who failed to get it right. St Michael's Church, Rock, says the card. But the locals would shake their heads. It should read St Michael's Church, Porthilly. When the emigrant ships were about to sail from Padstow, it was a tradition to come over across the estuary to St Michael's to pray for a safe journey to the New World.

A WEDDING RECEPTION at Rock Hotel, believed to be 1918 or 1919. J.B. Tucker's stores are in the background. The cars, suitably decorated for the wedding day, are all pre-war. The front car belonged to Mr L.G. Harris of Wadebridge, with him in attendance. This old car was built in 1906, and in 1909 it did the run from Peking, China to Paris, France. Incredibly in 1989 – precisely 80 years after that first run – it did the same journey from Peking to Paris. Its registration number was BY 36, and around 1912 Itala ceased production, a name long forgotten (except among old car enthusiasts), and not to be confused with Ital, produced by British Leyland in the late 1970s.
◀

PORT ISAAC from the air: probably an early airborne picture postcard. A far cry from the days, long ago, when the fishermen's cottages came steeply down the hill until they reached the Tudor quay and the breakwater. Fishing still goes on here and for many visitors Port Isaac remains a popular seaside village.
▼

Incoming Tide, Polzeath.

8/83

THIS MAGNIFICENT photograph of the Telegraph *at Port Isaac was taken by Herbert Hughes in June 1906. Mr Hughes, a mining engineer in the collieries, made photographic visits to Cornwall in the early years of this century. Like all the talented early visiting photographers to Cornwall, he was drawn like a magnet to the coastline. It is rather sad he and his colleagues ignored inland Cornwall and Bodmin Moor in particular. But this shot at low tide clearly demonstrates his eye and technique.*

I HAVE always loved photographs and photography. Here is a wonderful shot of an incoming tide at Polzeath. This photographer certainly had an eye for a good picture. Here the water, with the strength of the Atlantic behind it, comes thundering in – sometimes with the fury of a storm and at other times gently on a summer's day. Not many visitors know that Sabine Baring-Gould, the man who wrote that great hymn Onward Christian Soldiers, *set his novel* In the Roar of the Sea *in this part of North Cornwall; a story of dark nights and darker deeds, a combination of wrecking and plunder.*

A PEACEFUL picture by the quay at Padstow in 1910. LIttle did these children realize that four years later a terrible war would erupt against Germany. The war memorials in our villages and towns show how many Cornishmen we lost in those 1914-18 battles. And, of course, some of these boys probably donned service uniforms in 1939 when Hitler started yet another dreadful war.

49710   THE QUAY, PADSTOW, AN OLD PHOTO OF 1910.

COPYRIGHT
FRITH LTD

ANOTHER FACE of Padstow. This grand old photograph captures all the elegance of Edwardian days. This may have been some big sailing or social occasion, but the adults and the small boys seem to be mainly interested in conversation. It is nevertheless – and maybe because of that – a wonderfully evocative photograph. Old newspaper men said a good picture is worth a thousand words, and this photograph proves the point.

TWO MARVELLOUS old
photographs of the Padstow
Hobby Horse – or as many locals
put it 'Obby 'Oss. I love this great
day on the first of May in
Padstow: the wonder of it all,
that beat of the drum, and all
the colour … and to see all the
Padstow people uniting on this,
their day. The 'Obby 'Oss is a
fierce animal wearing a
fearsome mask. It is, in fact, an
man encased in black, save for
the coloured stripes on his cap
and mask. The horse, of course,
is a fertility symbol, and a young
woman who is 'caught' by the
'Oss, trapped under its skirts will,
according to age-old tradition,
become 'lucky' or pregnant. Old
Padstow people would run down
the street to avoid capture, but
today young women accept 'the
trapping' as a matter of sport.

44

THE FAMOUS
PADSTOW "HOBBY HORS

Padstow, Market Square

▲

HERE IS Padstow on another day, a quieter day in more leisurely times: Market Square. I have family links with the town. My uncle, a keen horseman, was at one time Town Crier, and my cousin and her husband ran a jewellers' shop in Mill Square. I often gave them a hand in the shop during the busy months of the summer – mind you sometimes, if it was really good weather, the town would be very quiet, with most of the visitors gone to the beach. I enjoyed my days working in Padstow, and travelled each morning from Wadebridge to Padstow by train, a beautiful run, and a lot of Wadebridge people, who worked in Padstow, would travel the same way. There would be quite a gang of us each morning.

NOT ONLY did the old photographers have a sharp, shrewd eye ▶ for a good photograph, they sometimes captured a bit of vanishing North Cornwall. Here is a good illustration. This old bridge crossing the road at Little Petherick has long since gone. I remember there was a manor house on the left, and you crossed the road above the traffic on this Wadebridge to Padstow road. There was a seat on the bridge where people would sit and watch the traffic travel beneath them. Through a magnifying glass it rather looks as if someone in white is waving to the photographer down on the road.

HARLYN BEACH from the Bridge. The photographer who took this shot knew the importance of a strong foreground subject. Take the old car out of this picture – and it loses a great deal of impact and interest.

THE MOVEMENT of the sea has fascinated and challenged painters and photographers in North Cornwall. Here a photographer responds to that challenge at Trevone: a skilful photographer, too, for he or she has used the figures on the beach. Their presence gives a sense of scale to the whole scene.

HARLYN BAY Prehistoric Settlement. Back in 1900 workmen sinking foundations for a dwelling uncovered caskets containing human bones. It proved to be one of the richest discoveries of prehistoric remains ever made in Britain – Celtic burials which probably took place 2500 years ago. Our rare old postcard shows relics being recovered from the sand.

HARLYN BAY PREHISTORIC SETTLEMENT, E. V. Bellers
Near PADSTOW, NORTH CORNWALL. REDDIE MALLETT, Proprietor. 1897

Recovering Relics from the Sand.

HERE IS a dramatic photograph: the shipwreck of the trawler Smiling Through at Harlyn in 1929. The onlookers give some idea of the size of the trawler. Our North Cornwall coast had a notorious reputation with sailors: littered with wrecks.

CONSTANTINE BAY provides a glorious stretch of sand, but, as almost anywhere along this north coast, bathers need to take care – and heed local guidance about where and when not to venture into the water. Here in the top photograph a man, his horse and cart have come down to collect sand from the beach.

IN THE village the presence of the motor cycle and the three motor cars clearly indicate that tourism had already come to this part of Cornwall, but in recent years annual holiday visits by the then Prime Minister Margaret Thatcher gave North Cornwall tourism a tremendous boost. Her visits naturally meant coverage by television, radio and press. On these occasions her husband Denis, a former Rugby referee, enjoyed rounds of golf on the local course.

Constantine Bay.

The Village, Constantine Bay, near Trevose Head.

FRITH.
TVH. 14

S.W. Hotel, Padstow — Argull's Series

A PICTURE postcard shot of the SW Hotel, Padstow, later renamed The Metropole. The railway and the growth of tourism brought prosperity to Padstow – but also helped to change the character of the old seaport. Sir John Betjeman, in an early Bossiney title, now out of print, recalled: 'All our shopping was done in Padstow and we carried it over the links from the ferry. The higher the tide, the shorter the walk.' As a boy the former Poet Laureate spent happy boyhood holidays at Trebetherick on the other side of the estuary.

PADSTOW, ROCK village reads this caption – but it is wrong. Padstow is on one side of the estuary and Rock village on the other! Rock Hotel, shown in this photograph was demolished in 1976. Many will have nostalgic memories of holidays spent here, sailing and golf were the main attractions for the early visitors who came to Rock. The curious fact is Rock does not live up to its name. At low tide there is scarcely a rock in sight – only the wide expanse of golden sand.

THE OPENING of the railway line at Padstow Station in 1893. All the gentlemen are very formally dressed for the occasion, even to the extent of top hat or bowler. Two ladies are present, also wearing hats. The gathering must be a mixture of railway officials and local dignitaries. Though called an express, the run from Waterloo to Padstow, for many years, was virtually a day's journey.

ONE OF my photographs, taken from a transparency. The subject is Tremeer at St Tudy, the former residence of Major General Harrison. Once, in a party of four, I had the good fortune to be shown around the grounds by the gardener there – all those beautiful flowers, it was a memorable occasion. Major General Harrison brought the plants home from the Himalayas. Tremeer is reputed to be the birth place of the notorious Captain Bligh of the Bounty, *whom Charles Laughton played with such distinction on the cinema screen. Another interesting slice of St Tudy history is that the very first blood transfusion was carried out at Tremeer using sheep. The doctor was one Dr Lover who later went to the court of King Charles II.*

THIS IS a photograph I took in 1985: my late husband Jerry standing by the famous Jubilee Rock in the Parish of Blisland. Here is something from C.S. Gilbert's Historical Survey of 1820: The northern side of Blisland is composed of waste lands or commons in the midst of which stands a large rock called Pendrift formerly a logan stone, and which Norden observes, "was so equally balanced, that the winds could move it to and fro." It is now immovable, and measures nine feet and a half in length, four feet in breadth and two and a half thick. It has lately been ornamented by Mr John Rogers, of this Parish, in the following manner. On the front of the rock is seated Britannia, designed like the impression on the common coin. At her feet is a bee-hive and in the back around a ship in full sail; the emblems of industry and commerce. On another part are sculptured the Cornish arms. The regent's plume, the royal arms of England and a plough; emblematical of loyalty and agriculture dated 1810. The two other squares are ornamented with the arms of Boscawen and Molesworth, a trowel and compasses. There are two annual fairs at Blisland, one in the church town, on the Monday after September 22 and the other at Poundscawse in the same Parish on the last Monday in November.

◀ THE BLISLAND INN, photographed in 1900. It is now The Royal Oak. Blisland is well worth a visit. Here you will see the only village green in all Cornwall. On the other side of the green stands one of the most beautiful churches in the whole of the Westcountry. It is dedicated to St Protus and St Hyacinth – the latter Saint was a man, although today the name is usually used for girls. The village itself is set in some glorious countryside: a mixture of farm land and moorland.

LOOKING DOWN on St Tudy – until recent times one of those neglected villages of North Cornwall. A guide to North Cornwall, published thirty years ago, had nearly 300 locations – but not a single word about St Tudy! As for the Saint himself, James Mildren in his Saints of the South West *wrote: 'He was an active missionary, who founded monasteries on islands and rivers in the north and south of Brittany.' His feast is observed on the 11th day of May.*

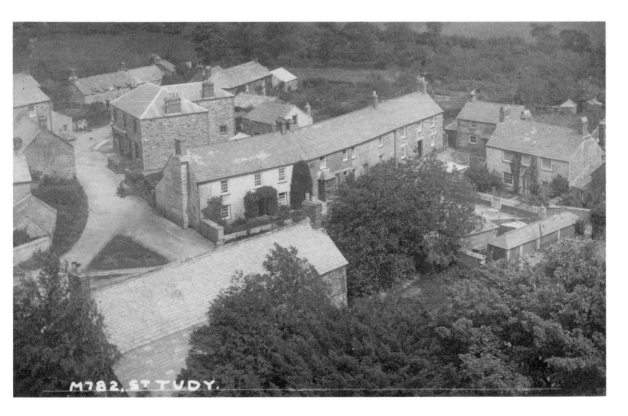

M782, ST TUDY.

A ROMANTIC 1914-1918 War picture postcard: 'Tender Thoughts for my Soldier Boy.' Such cards would have been sent by Cornish girls and young women to their 'Soldier Boys' in France.

A YOUNG MAN from St Tudy came home from the 1914-18 war with a conker which he had picked up in Flanders. This conker was planted near the memorial outside St Tudy Church and grew to be the magnificent tree that it is today. It has not only given great pleasure to generations of youngsters in the village, it is also a fitting tribute to those men who never returned home to North Cornwall.

St. Tudy Church, North Cornwall.

Published by J. E. Oatey, Wadebridge.

Launch of the Newquay Lifeboat

▲

Spectacular launch of the Newquay Lifeboat witnessed by a gathering of onlookers. Ethel, who sent this card to Mrs Myers of 77 Regent Street, Plymouth, in August 1912, is not happy: 'Arrived safe but it is very dirty weather here ...'

▶

NEWQUAY WAS once a tiny fishing village but has grown into a large town and is today a major holiday resort in Cornwall. This grand old photograph was taken in the days when sailing vessels used the harbour. As tourism grew in Cornwall, Newquay quickly became a favourite choice for family holidays: the glorious sands ideal for the children and lovely coastal walks for the adults and for those who needed bracing air, Newquay, facing the Atlantic, had the edge on resorts on the south coast.

Below:
THE MAJESTY of steam: a train crosses the Trenance Viaduct Newquay. Despite threats of cuts in railway services in the Westcountry, this Newquay line remains in operation.

Trenance Viaduct, Newquay.

St. Columb, Market
House & "King's Arms".

Bank Square, St. Columb

Argall's Series

*ST COLUMB remains a stronghold of the ancient Cornish sport
of hurling which many believe was the ancestor of our modern
game of Rugby. St Columb was also the birthplace of Jack
Crapp, the first Cornishman to play cricket for England in a test
match. These cards have nothing to do with sport, but they show
St Columb in more leisurely days – there is not a car in sight!
The top left card is of the Market House and the King's Arms.
There are in fact two St Columbs – these cards relate to St
Columb Major which for many years was one of the most
serious traffic problem areas in North Cornwall – see the
narrow streets! But today St Columb Major is bypassed by a fast
modern road. St Columb minor is a village between St Columb
Major and Newquay. Many years ago a young boy called Ralph
Allen sped around the village with letters while staying with his
grandmother who ran the village post office. Little did he or his
grandmother dream that he would make a fortune by carrying
letters, and would spend it making the city of Bath famous
throughout the world. Ralph Allen was the Cornishman who
made vast sums out of the Post Office by carrying mails, and
spending much of his fortune by giving the Woods – architects,
father and son – the chance to use their talents and vision.
The card above shows Mr Jack Rowe with his horse and cart at
Town Mills Bridge, St Columb and bottom left, a quiet and
deserted Bank Square.*

▲

THE QUEEN Bess Rock at Bedruthan Steps. This was a popular Cornish postcard subject. It was posted from St Columb to Miss Michell of Trethewell, St Just, St Mawes via Falmouth in 1904 and the message is 'Dear A, Got back alright. Had a nice time at Truro. It is very wet here today. I am very well. With love to all. M.M.'

THE ROYAL Air Force was very active here in North Cornwall during the war years. In addition to air stations in St Mawgan and St Eval, the Americans built an airfield on Davidstow Moor – a disastrous choice because of frequent fog. This unusual card is of a "Buffalo 1" Fighter Plane, single seater with retracting undercarriage. The card was, in fact, passed by the Press and Censorship Bureau and was part of the 'Britain Prepared' series.

BODMIN PARISH Church. Dedicated to St Petrock, it is the largest parish church in the Westcountry. The Saint, who arrived at Bodmin in the 6th century, is said to have sailed from Ireland in a coracle – or a silver dish – or a millstone. Anyway St Petroc came on to Bodmin, and St Guron, a hermit – after whom the well is named – obligingly moved on, and the Saint founded his famous monastery ▶

'BUFFALO 1" FIGHTER PLANE, SINGLE SEATER WITH RETRACTING UNDERCARRIAGE   "BRITAIN PREPARED" 46

BODMIN PARISH CHURCH
(ST PETROCK)

This is the largest Parish Church in the West of England and is dedicated to St. Petrock who arrived in Bodmin in the 6th century. He is said to have sailed from Ireland in a coracle to Padstow, other stories say a silver dish and a mill-stone. On his arrival in Bodmin, St. Guron, a hermit (after whom the well is named) obligingly moved on and our saint founded his famous monastery and for about 300 years Bodmin was a great power in the ecclesiastical world.

St. Petrock arriving in the Camel Estuary at Padstow.

*FORE STREET, Bodmin, at
the turn of the century. A
quiet scene here, but this
would often have been a busy
place, country people coming
in from the moorland villages
to do their shopping and
often lots of soldiers about
too, for Bodmin was the
headquarters of the Duke of
Cornwall's Light Infantry.
The Assizes, then based at
Bodmin, would have brought
extra business – and people –
to the town.*

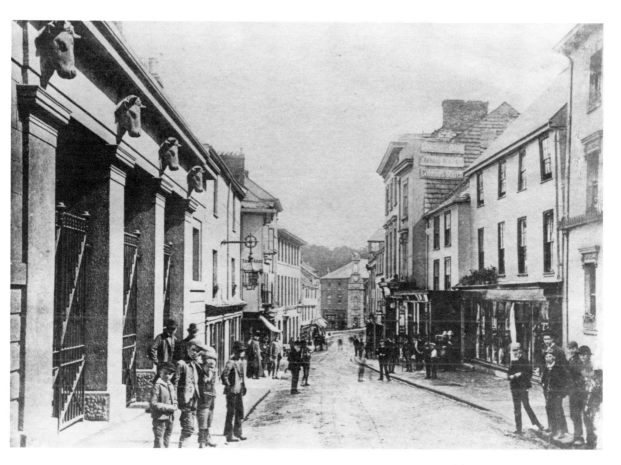

ANOTHER PHOTOGRAPHER looks down Fore Street, getting a good shot of people and the clock tower lower down the street. This was clearly a busier day and it's interesting to see how so many people posed for the photographer. Today a photographer in the street would be virtually ignored.

FROM ~
GHOULIES &

GHOSTIES & LONG LEGGETTY · BEASTIES
AND · THINGS · THAT · GO · BUMP · IN · THE · NIGHT.
GOOD · LORD · DELIVER · US.

NORTH CORNWALL has a haunted reputation. There is scarcely a village without a ghost. These picture postcards, of course, are intended to amuse, entertain and perhaps frighten. But there is no doubt many people in North Cornwall have seen and heard things which have defied all logical explanation. Both cards contain an old Cornish Litany.

A CORNISH LITANY.
FROM GHOULIES
AND GHOSTIES,
AND LONG-LEGGETTY
BEASTIES,
AND THINGS THAT GO
BUMP IN THE NIGHT,
GOOD LORD DELIVER US.

A LYRICAL shot of Beacon Hill, high above the town of Bodmin: cattle grazing quietly and people enjoying the views. The granite column, rising 144 feet, is in memory of a brave soldier in the Sikh Wars who died after the Mutiny. He bore the proud name of Sir Walter Raleigh Gilbert, for he belonged to the family of celebrated Humphrey Gilbert, stepbrother of Sir Walter Raleigh. Bodmin's Beacon Hill and the GIlbert Obelisk can be seen for miles and miles.

CATS HAVE long been a favourite subject for photographers. Here is an appealing card from the Edwardian reign. Of course we Cornish are often very superstitious. The Romanies always rated a black cat as a sign of good luck – and on seeing a black cat would put a wish on it – this therefore would have been a strong selling card in its day. Students of the supernatural believe too that cats are among the most psychic of animals.

LET ME BE YOUR MASCOT

THE NAME Altarnun means 'The Altar of St Nonna,' a Cornish saint, patron also of a Breton parish. Church experts rate the pew ends as 'the greatest treasures' of this church. There are 79 of them – here are just some examples of this rich carving.

Altarnon Church.   Bench Ends. 1530.

SOME MAY quibble over my putting Liskeard inside the pages of North Cornwall Reflections. It's true Liskeard isn't inside the North Cornwall political constituency, but many of us feel it's the eastern edge of North Cornwall, certainly a town which serves Bodmin Moor. Here, anyway, is a card of Barras Street and Parade, Liskeard: not a motor car in sight! 'A little town between the valleys with steep and narrow streets ...' was how Arthur Mee saw it when he came to Cornwall in the 1930s. Of course, it's grown in the last 60 years and a by-pass to Plymouth now reduces the traffic congestion of the town. Robert Stephen Hawker was educated here – as was Dr John Wolcot, the writer who discovered John Opie, the Cornish portrait painter.

Liskeard, Barras Street & Parade.

Southgate Arch, Launceston.

THE SOUTHGATE Arch, Launceston, must be one of the most photographed spots in the whole of North Cornwall. This picture postcard dates from the times when a sycamore tree grew out of the masonry. In those days the shop on the right was Jesse Raddall's saddler's shop. Not a traffic warden in sight when the photographer came to take this photograph! For many Cornish people it remains a special thrill to travel through the Southgate Arch.

215 H.M. THE KING DURING THE CORONATION CEREMONY SURROUNDED BY THE KNIGHTS OF THE BATH IN HENRY VII. CHAPEL AT WESTMINSTER ABBEY. 22ND JUNE, 1911.

IT IS AN interesting fact that some postcards depicting national events come into Cornish collections. Here is one such example: King George V during the Coronation ceremony surrounded by the Knights of the Bath in Henry VII Chapel at Westminster Abbey on June 22 1911. I would have been one year old at that time.

ANCIENT CEREMONY
became pageantry at
Launceston Castle in 1973
when Prince Charles received
his feudal dues as the Duke
of Cornwall. A brace of
greyhounds rendered by Lt
Col J.A. Molesworth-St Aubyn
were in fact loaned by Ralph
Parsons of Wadebridge. Our
photograph shows the Duke
getting to know Rising Peak
and Rew Prederys. Looking
on behind Mr Parsons are Joy
Pardoe and her husband
John, the then Liberal MP for
Cornwall. More than three
thousand people assembled
in the grounds of the
Norman Castle.

WITHIEL IS one of those neglected, almost forgotten, Cornish villages. Here is a rare picture postcard of the village only a few miles from Bodmin. On the left is one of those solid telephone boxes which have disappeared from our streets. Sir Bevil Grenville, a great Royalist in the Civil War, spent a good deal of his boyhood hereabouts. Sir Bevil fell with a letter from the king in his pocket, during the Battle of Lansdowne Hill, Bath in the summer of 1643. Earlier he had led the Royalists to a famous victory near Bude.

WITHIEL VILLAGE, NEAR BODMIN.

C. 2170.

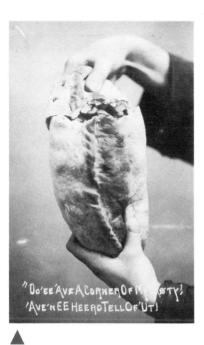

▲

THE FIRST Cornish pasties came on to the cooking scene towards the end of the eighteenth century, made 'for the lower orders'. However over the years the pasty has grown into a perfect moveable feast. The Cornish miners often had meat and vegetables at one end, and apples and cream at the other – with the miner's initial on the far right hand corner, so that he could put it down and be sure of picking up his own pasty again when he wanted to eat it.

▲

THOSE EARLY photographers in North Cornwall – and everywhere else – were always on the lookout for characters. Here is one such character Dickie Craddock who sold snides and handpins for scythes.

THIS LADY's face is full of character. She was Mrs Mary Roose who lived in the Mill at Polmorla: a very popular local character in her day.

A regular sprinkle of

HARPIC

cleans and disinfects the lavatory-pan in one operation

Sold in
6d., 1/- and 1/9 tins

HARPIC cleans without labour, kills the germs in the bend of the pipe where the brush cannot reach, and removes the cause of odours.

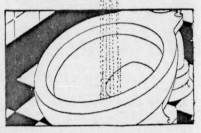

HARPIC MFG. CO. LTD., HULL AND LONDON

MACFARLANE LANG'S
"STANDARD ASSORTED"

BISCUITS

HALF TINS AS ILLUSTRATED

$3\frac{1}{4}$ lbs.
weight

4/4 Tin

RETURNABLE TIN
8d. extra

GROCERIES

ALMONDS.		s.	d.
Jordan ..	per lb	2	0
Valencia ..	,,	2	0
Ground, Finest	,,	2	0 .
Bitter ..	,,	2	3
Almond Substitute	,,	1	6

AMMONIA.			
Scrubb's ..	per bot.	1	4

ANCHOVIES.			
Three-ring	..	1	3
Hotel Size, in Olive Oil	..	5	3

ANCHOVY PASTE.
See Potted Meats.

ANCHOVY ESSENCE.
See Sauces.

ANGELICA.			
Per lb 3/6 ..	per oz.	0	3

APRICOTS.
Dried. See Dried Fruits.

ARROWROOT. Per lb ..		1	6

ASPARAGUS. See Vegetables.

ALLENBURY'S.			
Food No. 3 per tin 1/3 and		2	6
Rusks ..	per tin	2	3

APPLES.			
Per gallon tin	..	2	6
Per 4's size ..	..	0	11½

BAKING POWDER.			
Borwick's tin 7½d., 1/3 and		3	2
Royal per tin 7½d. and		1	2
Breezes ..	per tin	0	7½
Beechwood per 1-lb tin		0	10½
Loose ..	per lb	0	9

BARLEY.			
Finest Pearl ..	per lb	0	4
Robinson's Patent per tin 7½d. and		1	3
Barley Kernels per pkt.		0	8
Clark's Creamed per pkt. 7½d. and		1	2

BATH CUBES.			
Reckitt's per box 6 cubes		0	10½

BATH BRICKS.			
Each ..	..	0	2
Drums, Powder	each	0	2

BEANS.			
Butter Beans ..	per lb	0	5½
Haricots ..	,,	0	4
Baked Beans. See Heinz.			

BIRD SEED.		s.	d.
Spratt's Parrot Food per pkt. 6d. and		1	0
Spratt's Bird Seed per pkt.		0	6
Pearce Duff's ,,		0	3½
Spratt's Bird Sand ..		0	2
Spratt's Budgerigar Seed per pkt.		0	6

BEEF. See Provisions.

BLANCO.			
White ..	per tin	0	6
Refills ..	..	0	2

BISTO.			
Per drum 3d.	per pkt.	0	7½
Per tin ..	..	0	10½

BORAX. Refined.			
Powder ..	per lb	0	8

BROWNING. Gravy.			
Heinz .. 6d. and		0	10½
Rayner's 7½d., 10½d. and		1	6
Brand's ..			

BOVRIL.			
1-oz. jar 7½d.	2-oz. jar	1	2
4-oz. jar 2/1½	8-oz. jar	3	9
16-oz. jar ..	..	6	2

BRUNSWICK BLACK.			
Per tin ..	..	0	10½

BENGER'S FOOD.			
Per tin 1/4, 2/3 and		4	0

BEANS.			
C. & B.'s ..	per tin	0	4
Heinz 3d., 5d. and		0	10½
Heinz Curried	..	0	6

BRAND'S PREPARATIONS.			
Essence of Beef	per tin	2	6
Essence of Chicken	,,	2	9

BLUE.			
Reckitt's ..	square	0	1
4 squares for		0	3½

BI-CARBONATE SODA.			
Per lb ..	..	0	6
Drums ..	..	0	2

BLACK LEAD.			
Enameline ..	per tin	0	3
Zebra ..	,,	0	3
Rising Sun ..	..	0	3
Zebo Liquid tin 4d., 6d. and		0	9
Domeleine ..	..	0	3

L. CHAPMAN & Sons was a grocer's shop with three or four vans out on the roads. It was based in Glen Road, Wadebridge – now an off-licence. I suspect that these prices are 50 years out of date.

MR MUNCEY's electric shop in Park Road, about 1970. At one time a lady called Mrs Nancarrow had a very good clothing store here and employed five girls back in the 1930s. During the first World War the building was used as a Calvinist Church because there were many Dutch and Belgian refugees living in Wadebridge – and Calvinism had been the religion of their homelands. As far as I know none of them remained in Cornwall. After the war they all went back to Holland and Belgium.

HERE IS the commercial face of old North Cornwall. This photograph outside the North Cornwall Boot Company shows the owner, Mr Crab, with his young son and Mr Paul who later opened his own shoe shop in Molesworth Street. Standing in the lower doorway are Mrs Crab and Miss Taylor.

J.E. OATEY was the well-known Wadebridge photographer. I remember going there as a small child with my aunt from Padstow who had her daughter's photograph taken here. You went through the shop and up several steps to his studio. His old postcards are now quite expensive to buy – and much in demand.

THIS EASILY-recognisable photograph of what we know as Belmont Auction Rooms shows the building may not have changed much structurally, but how many people remember that it was once Mr Opie's Temperance Hotel and restaurant? The dentist, Mr Creeper would come one day a week from Plymouth to pull the teeth of local sufferers at his surgery here. The general stores on the right of the picture were demolished before I came to live in the area in 1924. It belonged to Captain Ball, a retired naval gentleman, who later had a wonderful fish and chip shop on the Platt where Aston's carpets are today.

CLEARLY SCHOOL photographs were a serious business – not a single smile for the photographer. These girls attended the Wadebridge Junior School and the photograph was taken during the first war, probably in the year 1916.

A GLIMPSE of old Wadebridge: the level crossing gates and what is now Lang's fish and chip shop. Then it was a Temperance Hotel. Young people today may find it hard to believe that back in the Victorian and Edwardian times many men and women would have nothing to do with 'strong drink' and refused to patronise establishments with bars.

To the Electors of the New Parish of Wadebridge.

Ladies and Gentlemen,

Having been solicited, and requested to offer myself as a Candidate for a GUARDIAN OF THE POOR of the New Parish of Wadebridge, in the Bodmin Poor Law Union, I trust you will be good enough to give me your support and interest on the Polling Day, MONDAY, APRIL 4th.

My actions and attendance for over three years on the St. Columb Board of Guardians and Rural District Council—every Meeting of which I have attended, and taken a very active part in—are well known, and I believe approved of by the majority of Electors.

THE WADEBRIDGE URBAN DISTRICT COUNCIL, I also offer my services to the Electors.

To be on this Council is my desire and choice, having been one of the first promoters, and having taken a leading part in bringing it to maturity.

It is now to be hoped you will elect 15 good men, who have the well being and prosperity of Wadebridge at heart.

Pure Water must have the first and immediate attention.

Plans, estimates, and applications for borrowing money have already been forwarded to the Local Government Board. It will be the duty of the new Board to see that the money is borrowed on the best terms possible, and that the work be carried out expeditiously and with economy.

Another important matter for the new Council will be to see that the Highways are taken over in a 'proper condition, also that the best terms are made for Lighting, and last but very important, Sanitation and Drainage. The latter should be taken in detail, and done in sections as required. With proper and judicious care, the rates should not be increased so as to become oppressive.

Trusting you will vote for me and use your interest on my behalf, and return 14 other good and true men, on MONDAY, APRIL 4th.

Yours faithfully,

W. H. CRAIG.

Wadebridge,
    March 24th, 1898.

MRS MABEL Philp, aged 90, sitting by her Oatey and Martin's kitchen range. She was a neighbour and good friend of mine in Edyystone Terrace; we would often chat by that fire. She died at the grand age of 102, and remained very alert until the last few weeks of her life. I remember taking her an old photograph only a matter of weeks before the end, and she was able to recall things in detail. A truly wonderful lady.

A PHOTOGRAPHIC memory of the Hitler War: sand bags outside Wadebridge Town Hall, and the Co-operative shop boarded up in case of German air raids. In reality Cornwall did not suffer heavily from German bombers – unlike Plymouth across the Tamar which was the victim of a massive blitz. Many Cornish people, recalling the war years, remember seeing red sky at night as Plymouth burned. I was living in Wellington Place at the time, and I can still remember the night when the Germans dropped three bombs in the field above us, you could hear the bombs whistling. Nobody was killed and no buildings were hit, but all our ceilings were cracked and later had to be repaired or replaced.

◄

A CANDIDATE seeks election in 1898 as a Poor Law Guardian, responsible for administering relief and admitting the destitute to the workhouse, and also as a Wadebridge Urban District Councillor – promising, as ever, many amenities without too much burden on the ratepayer.

THESE TWO photographs show how Wadebridge suffered during the floods of July 14 1965. The top photograph is the clearing up operation in Molesworth Street. Firemen and many local inhabitants worked all night to clear the terrible mess which had been caused by a cloud burst. The lower photograph shows Riversdale, another part of the town, suffering from the same fate. There had been a cloud burst at White Rock and the water came pouring down the hill into the town – also down into the church. The Army came with driers and they worked wonders drying out the houses.

HERE IS the cast of Puss in Boots presented by Megan Brown as a 'Grand Family Pantomime' at the Town Hall Wadebridge in January 1954. Writing in the programme Mr J.J.B. Collicott said 'For this our first Pantomime, our producer has chosen "Puss in Boots", because it has a splendid "old time" story which she has cleverly adapted to delight young and old alike.' The cast included Pam Phillips, Jack Baragwaneth, Phyllis Julian, Ken Mitchell, Jack Palmer, Gladys Chapman, Jean Harris, Margaret Rowe, Mrs Tucker, Gloria Chapman, Eileen Eddy, Peggy Croft, Mary Scott, Marjorie Job, Irene Lucy, Joyce Chapman, Ron Chapman, Joan Paul, Ted Phillips, Pauline Reseigh, Mary Martyn, Amy Provins, Muriel Saunders, Iris Brenton, Stella Deverson, Lorne Scott, Gwyneth May, Mary Harris and Freda Hooper.

THIS AMBITIOUS pantomime, put on with the help of Dr Gunn's Orchestra, included nursery rhyme characters and more topical favourites such as Teddy Tail and Tiger Tim. The cast list included quite a few of the names which also featured in the 1954 Puss in Boots pictured on the preceding page so there was obviously a loyal core of enthusiasts involved. And it was all in a good cause – this 1933 production was for a Local Benevolent Fund.

Town Hall, Wadebridge,

MARCH 10th, 1933.

PROGRAMME OF
- PANTOMIME -
PETER BRAY and his A.B.C.

(Reproduced by special request)

Written by Mrs. F. E. PALMER.

Music by Mrs. M. PALMER.

Accompanist :—Mrs. K. FISHWICK.

Dr. GUNN'S ORCHESTRA.

Dresses by Members of Women's Section British Legion.

Proceeds in aid of Local Benevolent Fund.

PROGRAMME.

Overture ... ... Orchestra	Overture ... ... Orchestra
ACT I.	Interlude ... ... Mad Hatter
Scene I.—Peter Bray's School Room.	ACT II.
Scene II.—Peter's Night Nursery. *(Peter's first dream.)*	Scene I.—Peter's Night Nursery. *(Peter's second dream)*
✤ INTERVAL. ✤	Scene II.—Peter's Night Nursery.
	Finale.

GOD SAVE THE KING.

BACK IN 1900 the St Mabyn concert drew on local talent to provide a lively-sounding entertainment which cost two shillings for those in the best reserved seats, one shilling in the front and just sixpence for those crowded in at the back. Mr T. Kelly who started the proceedings with a violin solo appears to have involved the whole family later in the evening, there's a talented cleric who plays the piano and sings and others offer recitations and patriotic songs. The evening ends with a dance – gentlemen one shilling, ladies free.

✦ ST. MABYN CONCERT ✦

DECEMBER 6TH, 1900.

RESERVED SEATS, 2s. FRONT SEATS, 1s. BACK SEATS, 6d.

ALL RESERVED SEATS MUST BE BOOKED BY NOON ON DAY OF CONCERT.

PART 1.

1.	Violin Solo	"Heimliche."	J. Resche.
		MR. T. KELLY.	
2.	Song	"Out on the Deep."	Cowen.
		MR. CLIMO.	
3.	Song	"The Cautious Lover."	Corney Grain.
		MR. C. M. JAGGARD.	
4.	Duet	"The Battle Eve."	Bonheur.
		MESSRS. ENNOR & CREWS.	
5.	Pianoforte Solo	"Spinning Song."	
		REV. DR. COLLISSON.	
6.	Song	"The Cuckoo in the Orchard."	Brown.
		MRS. T. BEST.	
7.	Song	"Hulloa! Hulloa !! Hulloa !!!"	Le. Brun.
		MR. F. MALLETT.	
8.	Trio	"Ye Shepherds tell Me."	Mazzinghi.
		KELLY FAMILY.	
9.	Song	"Victoria Queen of our Nation."	Russell.
		MR. SKINNER.	
10	Song	"The Better Land."	Cowan.
		MISS L. FOURACRE.	
11.	Recitation	Selected.	
		MR. MALLINSON.	
12.	Song	"The Volunteer."	McGlennon.
		MR. W. C. CREWS.	
13.	Song	"Mrs. Kelly."	Leno.
		MR. W. G. TICKELL.	

PART 2.

1.	Violin Solo	"Modesty."	Alan Macey.
		MR. T. KELLY.	
2.	Song	"The Miner."	Lutton.
		MR. CLIMO.	
3.	Song	"The Careful Man."	Grossmith.
		MR. C. M. JAGGARD.	
4.	Duet	"The Night Attack."	Quentin.
		MESSRS. ENNOR & CREWS.	
5.	Song	Selected.	
		REV. DR. COLLISSON.	
6.	Song	"Riding on a Load of Hay."	
		MRS. T. BEST.	
7.	Song	"Gallery and Boxes."	Rudd.
		MR. W. G. TICKELL.	
8.	Quartette	"When Hands Meet."	Cris Pinsuti.
		KELLY FAMILY.	
9.	Song	"Let me like a Soldier fall."	Wallace.
		MR. SKINNER.	
10.	Song	"In the Chimney Corner."	Cowen.
		MISS L. FOURACRE.	
11.	Recitation	Selected.	
		MR. MALLINSON.	
12.	Song	"Welcome to the C. I. V's."	Cummings.
		MR. C. O. ENNOR.	
13.	Song	"In the Wash."	

From the "Messenger Boy" by permission of Geo. Edwards, Esq.

MR. F. MALLETT

GOD SAVE THE QUEEN.

A PUBLIC DANCE AT 10 P.M.

GENTLEMEN, 1s.   LADIES, Free.   For Tickets apply to J. F. REID.

**TOWN HALL,
WADEBRIDGE**

JANUARY 5th
to JANUARY 12th, 1955,
(inclusive)
nightly at 7.30

MATINEE
SATURDAY, JAN. 8th
at 2.30 p.m.

**WADEBRIDGE
AMATEUR MUSIC
AND DRAMATIC
SOCIETY**
(President:
J. H. B. COLLICOTT, Esq.)

in conjunction with the

**WADEBRIDGE TOWN
FOOTBALL CLUB**

present

**THE GRAND
FAMILY
PANTOMIME**

PRICE—SIXPENCE

N°. 604

SLEEPING *Beauty*

THIS FAMILY PANTOMIME was put on by the rather strange combination of the local amateur music and dramatic society and Wadebridge Town Football Club. Quite how the footballers figured isn't clear, they are unlikely to have been elves or fairy budgerigars. But the production clearly involved most of the town, the chairman's programme notes express thanks to the traders, Norman Cleave for the use of his showroom window for exhibiting photographs and Mr and Mrs Jenkins for the use of the Long-room of the Swan Hotel. The spinning wheel – a vital part of the Sleeping Beauty plot – was supplied by Chapman Bros of Molesworth Street. Costumes, hats and sound equipment were all provided by willing local people.

Characters

KING OF WADEBRIDGEIA	**Arthur Pope**
QUEEN OF WADEBRIDGEIA	**Gillian Lucey**
PRINCESS MARIGOLD (The Sleeping Beauty)	**Mary Lucey**
LORD CHAMBERLAIN	**Victoria Moore**
NOTHER BROOME (The Palace Sweeper)	**Margaret Collicott**
TILLY (The Royal Nurse)	**Megan Brown**
DAFFY } Under Nurse maids to Tilly DILLY }	**Ellis Baker** **Norman Derry**
PIP } Pages POP }	**Margaret Mitchell** **Valerie Scantlebury**
LILLA } Maids of Honour LOLA }	**Jayne Rickard** **Edwina Mercer**
WILLIE (The Royal Trumpeter)	**David Lightfoot**
PRINCE FLORIZEL	**Rosemary Brown**
TONI (Equerry to the Prince)	**Maureen Hicks**
AN OLD VILLAGER	**Dudley Halling**
A VERY ANCIENT VILLAGER	**Geoffrey Eddy**
QUEEN SUNBEAM (Queen of the Fairies)	**Margaret Johnston**
FAIRY ROSE	**Angela Rickard**
FAIRY LAVENDER	**Vivien Mercer**
FAIRY SNOWDROP	**Vivienne Rickard**
FAIRY FORGET-ME-NOT	**Margaret Gill**
FAIRY DAFFODIL	**Patricia Carrol**
FAIRY BLUEBELL	**Fay Derry**
FAIRY NETTLE (A Wicked Fairy)	**Sally Rickard**
HERALDS	**Brian Pearne, Albert Perring**

LADIES & GENTLEMEN OF THE COURT   Margaret Allen, Jennifer Cook, Ann Halling, Anne Mitchell, Ann Knowles, Pamela Davey, Sylvia Kestle, Margaret Lang, Jacqueline Williams.

FAIRIES   Judith Wills, Ann Lightfoot, Mary Spong, Sandra Axworthy, Cathryn Polkinghorne, June Saunders, Barbara Birch, Mabel Perring.

ELVES   Mary Westlake, Celia George, Moya Fowler, Phillip Harris, Barbara Lang, Janet Dyke, Vivienne Harris, Glynn Wilson.

GOBLINS   Roger Goodfellow, James Lucy, Michæl Bate, Michæl Smith, John Armstrong, Brian Chapman.

FAIRY BUDGERIGARS   Christine Rickard, Patricia Vernon, Beverley Wills, Jean Chesterton, Marilyn Cosburn, Susan Oatey.

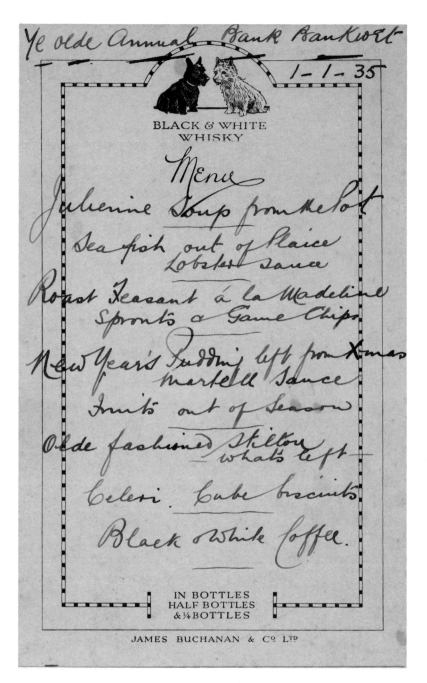

Ye olde Annual Bank Banket

1 - 1 - 35

BLACK & WHITE
WHISKY

Menu

Julienne Soup from the Pot

Sea fish out of Plaice
Lobster sauce

Roast Peasant á la Madeline
Sprouts & Game Chips

New Year's Pudding left from Xmas
Martell Sauce

Fruits out of Season

Olde fashioned Stilton
what's left

Celeri. Cube biscuits

Black & White Coffee.

IN BOTTLES
HALF BOTTLES
& ¼ BOTTLES

JAMES BUCHANAN & Cº LTD

A SUPPER MENU that bears closer inspection – perhaps for some club occasion at the start of 1935 – 'seafish out of plaice' is followed by 'New Year's pudding left from Xmas' and 'Olde fashioned Stilton – what's left' Where was this restaurant with a sense of humour?

MORE BOSSINEY BOOKS . . .

AROUND & ABOUT THE SMUGGLERS' WAYS
by David Mudd

Working through almost forty different sources, including the records of H.M. Customs & Excise itself, David Mudd (who discovered in the course of his research that his great-grandfather was a Customs officer) has produced a book that is as heady and addictive as the spirits, the wines and the tobaccos that once followed fish, tin and copper as Cornwall's great industries. Several of the sketches and many of the photographs are by David's wife, Diana.

'... scrapes the romantic glitter from Cornwall's erstwhile illicit trade ... Meticulously researched and written in David Mudd's lively factual style it makes absorbing reading.'

Alison Poole, Leader Group of Newspapers

MOUNT'S BAY
by Douglas Williams

In words and pictures Douglas Williams takes us from Land's End to Lizard Light, the most westerly and southerly point of Cornwall, enclosing a bay 'as majestic as any in Europe.'

DAPHNE DU MAURIER COUNTRY
by Martyn Shallcross

A special look at Cornwall in which the internationally-famous novelist set important stories.
'A treasure chest for those who love Cornwall and the du Maurier novels.'

Valerie Mitchell, The Packet Group of Newspapers

MY CORNWALL

A personal vision of Cornwall by eleven writers then living and working in the county: Daphne du Maurier, Ronald Duncan, James Turner, Angela du Maurier, Jack Clemo, Denys Val Baker, Colin Wilson, C.C. Vyvyan, Arthur Caddick, Michael Williams and Derek Tangye with reproductions of paintings by Margo Maeckelberghe.
'An ambitious collection of chapters.'

The Times, London

AROUND & ABOUT THE FAL
by David Mudd

'David Mudd's book brings to life the many aspects of one of Cornwall's most loved rivers.'

Sarah Foot, Cornish Scene

CASTLES OF CORNWALL
by Mary and Hal Price, 78 photographs and map.

St Catherine's Castle and Castle Dore both at Fowey, Restormel near Lostwithiel, St Mawes, Pendennis at Falmouth, St Michael's Mount, Tintagel, Launceston and Trematon near Saltash. Mary and Hal Price on this tour of Cornwall explore these nine castles.

'... a lavishly illustrated narrative that is both historically sound and written in a compelling and vivid style that carries the reader along from one drama to the next.'

Pamela Leeds, The Western Evening Herald

MYSTERIES IN THE CORNISH LANDSCAPE

by Tamsin Thomas of Radio Cornwall

A tour of thirty historic locations in Cornwall by the well-known Cornish broadcaster, starting at Chun Castle down in the Hundred of Penwith and ending at The Hurlers on the eastern edge of Bodmin Moor.

'Tamsin takes us on an enjoyable and speculative canter – literally for she is often on horseback – through these fascinating and often controversial features of old Kernow.'

Donald Rawe, Cornish Scene

'Tamsin has produced a delightful book which will enchant her audience.'

Ronnie Hoyle, The Western Morning News

KING ARTHUR COUNTRY in CORNWALL,
THE SEARCH for the REAL ARTHUR

by Brenda Duxbury, Michael Williams and Colin Wilson

Over 50 photographs and 3 maps

An exciting exploration of the Arthurian sites in Cornwall and Scilly, including the related legends of Tristan and Iseult, with The Search for the Real Arthur by Colin Wilson.

'... provides a refreshing slant on an old story linking it with the present.'

Caroline Righton, The Packet Newspapers

SUPERNATURAL SEARCH IN CORNWALL

by Michael Williams

DISCOVERING BODMIN MOOR

by E.V. Thompson

PARANORMAL IN THE WESTCOUNTRY

by Michael Williams

We shall be pleased to send you our catalogue giving full details of our growing list of titles from Devon, Cornwall, Dorset, Somerset and Wiltshire as well as forthcoming publications. If you have difficulty in obtaining our titles, write direct to Bossiney Books, Land's End, St Teath, Bodmin, Cornwall.

Back cover:
HORSE TRANSPORT in North Cornwall before the 1914-18 war. The driver on the right is Mr R. Andrews and the driver on the left is Mr A. Pinch. They are photographed on the former Launders Hill, Wadebridge. The ladies in the background look as if they are about to set off for a special outing.